THE IMPENDING GLEAM

Glen Baxter

JONATHAN CAPE
THIRTY BEDFORD SQUARE LONDON

To my parents

Also by Glen Baxter

THE FALLS TRACER
THE KHAKI
FRUITS OF THE WORLD IN DANGER
THE HANDY GUIDE TO AMAZING PEOPLE
CRANIREONS OV BOTYA
STORIES
THE WORKS
ATLAS

Many of the drawings in this book are
in private and public collections, including
those of the Arts Council of Great Britain
and the Victoria and Albert Museum.

First published 1981
Copyright © 1981 by Glen Baxter
Jonathan Cape Ltd, 30 Bedford Square, London WC1

British Library Cataloguing in Publication Data

Baxter, Glen
The impending gleam.
1. English wit and humor, Pictorial
I. Title
741.5′942   NC1479
ISBN 0 224 01992 9

Printed in Great Britain by St Edmundsbury Press Ltd
Bury St Edmunds, Suffolk

CONTENTS

WAY
OUT
WEST

PECOS BILL HAD A "THING"
ABOUT HOUSEHOLD DUST...

YOUNG ERIC HAD PREPARED HIMSELF FOR
ALMOST ANY EMERGENCY....

"I'VE CALLED ABOUT THE POST OF
ASSISTANT MILLINER" DRAWLED DEKE

"I PRUNE MY CHRYSANTHEMUMS THIS-A-WAY..."

Professions of the Old West
No. 2

The Dentist

"TO ME THE WINDOW IS STILL
A SYMBOLICALLY LOADED MOTIF"
DRAWLED CODY

"I MAKE A LIVING PEDDLING DANDRUFF"
SNORTED THE OLD TIMER

" SO YOU SEE, BOYS— WHAT A PICTURE MUST HAVE
IN COMMON WITH REALITY, IN ORDER TO BE
ABLE TO DEPICT IT — CORRECTLY OR INCORRECTLY
— IN THE WAY IT DOES, IS ITS PICTORIAL FORM"
EXPLAINED TEX

PANCHO'S SLEEPING ARRANGEMENTS WERE THE TALK
OF THE BUNKHOUSE

JEDSON WAS NOTED FOR HIS WITHERING
SIDELONG GLANCES

IT WAS TOM'S FIRST BRUSH WITH MODERNISM

"THE WAY I FIGGER IT — TRUTH <u>IS</u> UN-TRUTH INSOFAR AS THERE BELONGS TO IT THE RESERVOIR OF THE NOT-YET-REVEALED, THE UN-UNCOVERED IN THE SENSE OF CONCEALMENT" REASONED McTAGGART.

IT WAS THE HALITOSIS KID.....

"I KEEP MY BAGELS IN HERE" WHISPERED
THE DESPERADO

"I STUB MY CIGARS OUT.......THERE!"
SNORTED THE TEXAN

HE WAS FORCED TO ENDURE TERRIBLE
IMPERSONATIONS OF CATHY McGOWAN

YOUNG HANK ENTERTAINED THE BOYS
WITH A FINE DISPLAY OF SMOULDERING

AT THE GIVEN SIGNAL, MRS BOTHAM
POPPED OUT FROM THE CONCEALED
LINING AND BLASTED THE RATTLER

WILD BILL WAS KNOWN TO GO TO
EXTRAORDINARY LENGTHS TO CATCH
"THE LUCY SHOW" REPEATS ON CHANNEL 6

VANCE LIVED IN CONSTANT FEAR
OF LOSING HIS WRISTWATCH....

McGUIRE SEEMED TO HAVE RIDDEN INTO A
TRAP.....

THE LOMAX BOYS KEPT UP AN ALL-NIGHT
VIGIL ON THE NOUGAT

SETH TOOK HIS TEA AT SEVEN ON THE DOT

BIG JEB WAS A TRICKY CUSTOMER
ALLRIGHT

FRUITS OF THE WORLD
IN
DANGER

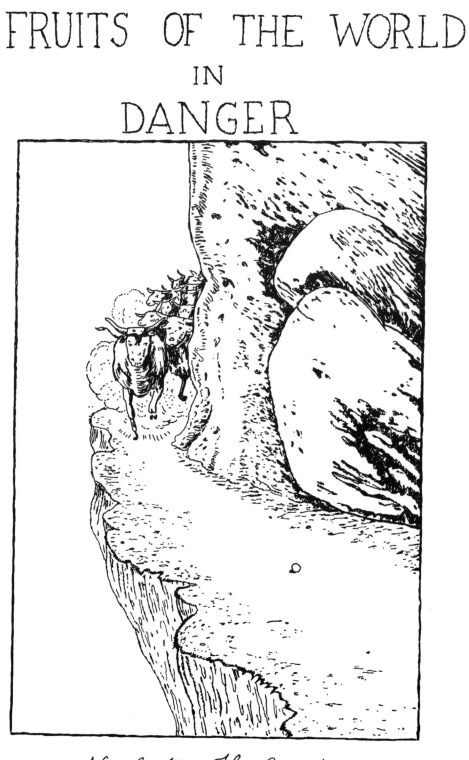

Number 10   The Apricot

"BUT SURELY, LANGUAGE IS NOT
DEFINED FOR US AS AN ARRANGE
-MENT FULFILLING A DEFINITE
PURPOSE..." STAMMERED JED.

HOW HE HATED SATURDAY MORNING SHOPPING

GREAT
MOMENTS
IN HISTORY
Number 43
The First Omelette

IT WAS A MONDAY AFTERNOON JUST LIKE
ANY OTHER.......

From the Pages of History

IT WAS A SMALL VOTIVE BUST
OF HELEN SHAPIRO.....

IT WAS THE SMALLEST PIZZA THEY HAD
EVER SEEN

"NOT SO FAST, VARLET — I DEMAND A SECOND
FITTING!" BELLOWED SIR PEREGRINE

ROBIN WAS CERTAINLY IMPRESSED
WITH THE SIMULATED TEAK FINISH

YOUNG ARTHUR'S EARRINGS WERE
THE TALK OF NOTTINGHAM

FRUITS OF THE WORLD
IN
DANGER

Number 12   The Kumquat

SIR ROLAND TRIED TO CONVINCE THE
SCEPTICS OF THE POTENTIAL OF HIS
LIGHTWEIGHT "MINI-SHIELD".......

"WHAT HAVE YOU DONE WITH MY WIMPLE?"
GROWLED BIG 'BULL' HARPER

IT WAS HUNGARIAN COOKING
ALLRIGHT.....

IT WAS HORRIBLE. FROM MY VANTAGE POINT I COULD
SEE THE STRUGGLING FIGURES BEING CARTED INTO
PROFESSOR TREMBO'S STRUCTURALIST FILM SEMINAR

HE TOOK HER IN HIS ARMS AND
GENTLY SQUEEZED HER GOATEE

"AH YES, MR. WRIGGLESWORTH — IT'S ABOUT THIS.... AHEM .... FIRST DRAFT OF YOUR NOVEL" SPLUTTERED MR. SCELPE

THE TWO MEN WERE IN AGREEMENT
— IT WAS A WORK OF SOME MERIT

THE TWO MEN WERE IN AGREEMENT
—IT WAS A WORK WITHOUT MERIT

FRUITS OF THE WORLD
IN
DANGER

Number 1   The Orange

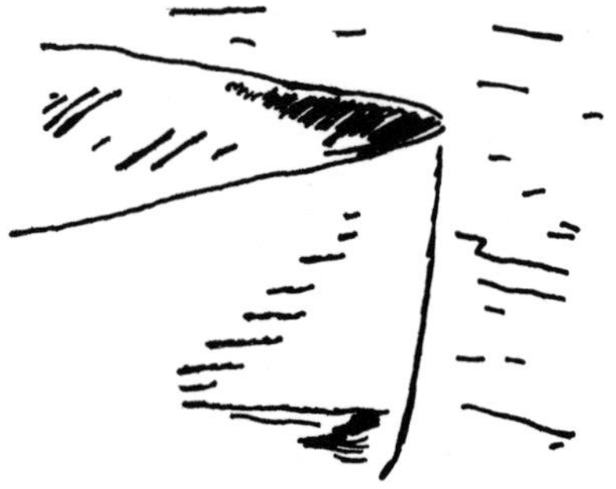

" I SENSED THAT BRENDA WAS TRYING
TO IMPRESS ME....."

AFTER TEA, MONICA WAS FORCED TO ENACT
THE GRIM RITUAL OF "COUNTING THE STUMPS"

DEIDRE POINTED OUT HER SUPPLY OF HASHISH
FOR THE AUTUMN TERM

ANGELA ADDRESSED THE MEMBERS OF
THE CROCHET CLUB ON HER PROPOSALS
FOR DEALING WITH LATECOMERS

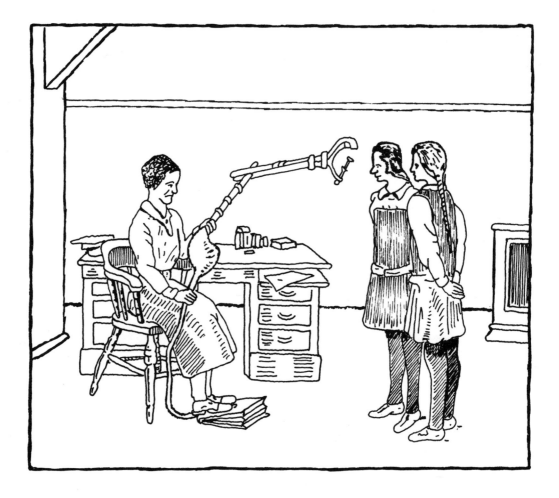

MISS FROBISHER MADE A POINT OF
THREATENING NEW ARRIVALS WITH
"THE NOSE TWEAKER"

MIRANDA HAD STUMBLED UPON OUR
SUPPLY OF BEARDS.....

IT HAD BEEN SUSPECTED FOR SOME TIME
THAT MAVIS WAS EXPERIMENTING WITH A
COMBINATION OF BALKAN AND TURKISH BLENDS

DAPHNE BEGAN TO SENSE SHE WAS NO
LONGER ALONE.......

"GOING DOWN TO THE VILLAGE AGAIN, EH?" SNAPPED MADGE

BERYL HAD HIT UPON A WAY OF RELIEVING
THE TEDIUM OF MISS ABERGHAST'S LESSONS

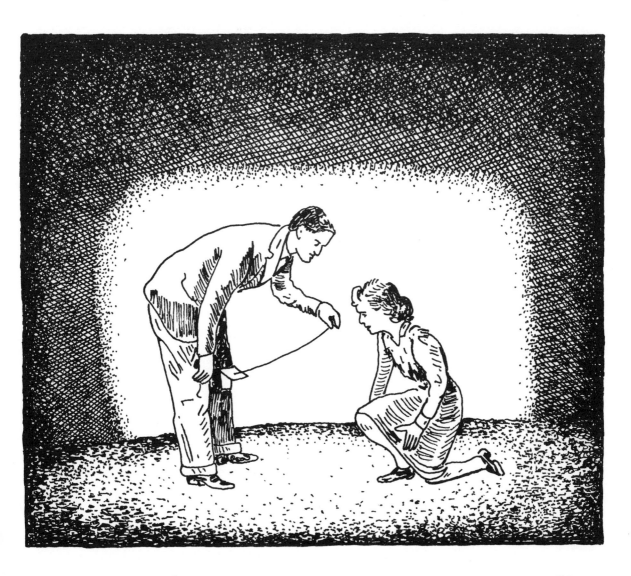

HE WAS FROM BROOKLYN ALLRIGHT

GREAT FAILURES OF OUR TIME

Nº 160

The First Pencil Sharpener

"SO YOU'RE THE MYOPIC MULDONI BOYS FROM CHICAGO, EH?" SPAT LANNIGAN

THE NURSE ENTERED WITH THE
BRIGADIER'S CALORIE-CONTROLLED
BREAKFAST....

GUSTAV'S NEON WIMPLE WAS CLEARLY
FAILING TO IMPRESS THELMA

"SOME ARE HAM AND SOME ARE CHEESE AND PICKLE" CONFIDED PANDOWSKI

"I SUPPOSE YOU'RE ALL WONDERING WHY I'VE GATHERED YOU HERE TODAY" WHISPERED THE BOSUN

IT WAS THE FOURTH TIME THAT DADDY HAD
FALLEN FOR THE EXPLODING FORK ROUTINE...

THERE WAS A HINT OF TRIUMPH
IN UNCLE FRANK'S BLUE EYES

THERE WAS GENUINE CONCERN IN
DAPHNE'S FRANK BLUE EYES

HE WAS NOT THE MAN SHE
HAD LOVED THAT EVENING
IN BRIDGEPORT.....

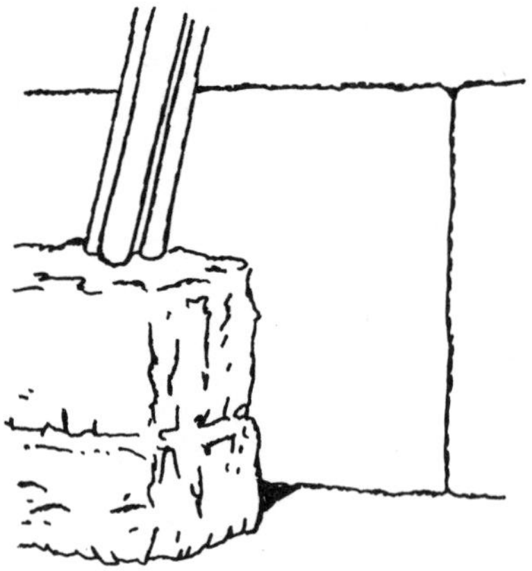

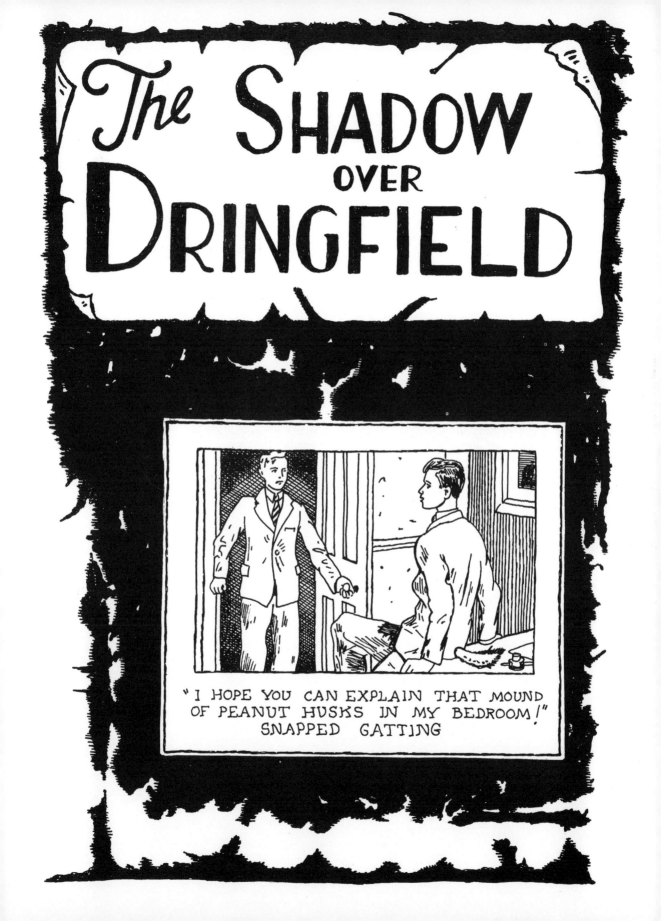

The Shadow over Dringfield

"I HOPE YOU CAN EXPLAIN THAT MOUND OF PEANUT HUSKS IN MY BEDROOM!" SNAPPED GATTING

"THERE'S ONLY ONE WAY TO
EAT WHELKS" HISSED GREIG

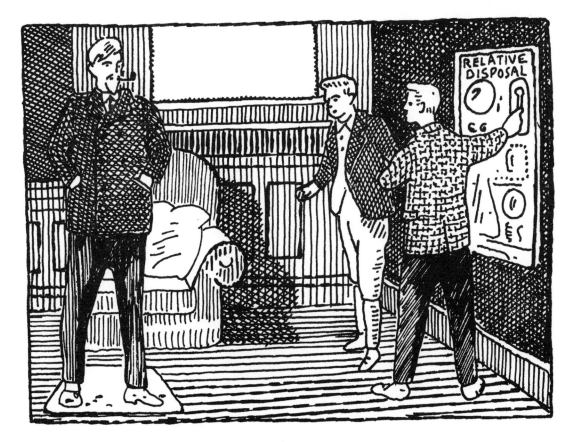

THE LADS HAD A WAY OF DEALING
WITH BORING OLD RELATIVES

"I'M AFRAID IT'S GRIM NEWS, SANDY—
THE VICE-CONSUL INTENDS TO BAN
THE WEARING OF WIMPLES AFTER 7·15 P.M"

"WHEN THIS IS SWITCHED ON, YOUR
PANTS WILL BE CLEANED AND PRESSED
EVERY TWO MINUTES" SNAPPED TOWLE

SUNDAYS CAME AROUND WITH
DEPRESSING REGULARITY

THERE WAS STILL MUCH TO
LEARN ABOUT SZECHUAN
CUISINE.....

IT WAS A DEVICE FOR TURNING SCHOOL MEALS
BACK INTO FOOD

" IF THERE HAS BEEN A MISHAP ON THE SPORTS FIELD THEN NATURALLY I WANT TO BE THE FIRST TO KNOW " MUMBLED THE HEADMASTER

WITH AN AIR OF WEARIED RESIGNATION
PROFESSOR COOMBES TUCKED THE ESSAY
BACK INTO MY BEARD

HE HAD BEEN CAUGHT USING THE
FORBIDDEN "HEAD-PEN" AGAIN.....

"BUT......I...ORDERED THE
CHICKEN KIEV..." BLURTED COOPER

"I'LL THANK YOU TO STOP JUGGLING MY GHERKINS!"
SNORTED THE ANGUISHED THROGUE

"NOW WHICH ONE OF YOU IS MRS. BLOYARD?"
ASKED THE INSPECTOR

BARTWELL SAW THROUGH THE DISGUISE
ALMOST IMMEDIATELY

HAMMOND OUTLINED THE RUDIMENTS
OF HIS DARING ESCAPE PLAN

ESSENTIAL SUPPLIES WERE DROPPED
TO THE BRITISH AGENTS....